Foals

By Nicole Horning

Cavendish
Square

New York

Published in 2021 by Cavendish Square Publishing, LLC
243 5th Avenue, Suite 136, New York, NY 10016

Copyright © 2021 by Cavendish Square Publishing, LLC

First Edition

Website: cavendishsq.com

This publication represents the opinions and views of the author based on his or her personal experience, knowledge, and research. The information in this book serves as a general guide only. The author and publisher have used their best efforts in preparing this book and disclaim liability rising directly or indirectly from the use and application of this book.

All websites were available and accurate when this book was sent to press.

Library of Congress Cataloging-in-Publication Data

Names: Horning, Nicole, author.
Title: Foals / Nicole Horning.
Description: First edition. | New York : Cavendish Square Publishing, [2021] | Series: Baby animals in action! | Includes index.
Identifiers: LCCN 2019059383 (print) | LCCN 2019059384 (ebook) | ISBN 9781502656117 (library binding) | ISBN 9781502656094 (paperback) | ISBN 9781502656100 (set) | ISBN 9781502656124 (ebook)
Subjects: LCSH: Foals–Juvenile literature.
Classification: LCC SF302 .H65 2021 (print) | LCC SF302 (ebook) | DDC 636.1–dc23
LC record available at https://lccn.loc.gov/2019059383
LC ebook record available at https://lccn.loc.gov/2019059384

Editor: Nicole Horning
Copy Editor: Nathan Heidelberger
Designer: Deanna Paternostro

The photographs in this book are used by permission and through the courtesy of: Cover Katho Menden/Shutterstock.com; p. 5 pfluegler-photo/Shutterstock.com; p. 7 Katrin-ps/Shutterstock.com; p. 9 acceptphoto/Shutterstock.com; p. 11 Geza Farkas/Shutterstock.com; p. 13 shymar27/Shutterstock.com; p. 15 Victoria Rak/Shutterstock.com; p. 17 arthorse/Shutterstock.com; p. 19 OlesyaNickolaeva/Shutterstock.com; p. 21 Natalia Deksbakh/Shutterstock.com; p. 23 Vasyl Syniuk/Shutterstock.com.

Some of the images in this book illustrate individuals who are models. The depictions do not imply actual situations or events.

CPSIA compliance information: Batch #CS20CSQ: For further information contact Cavendish Square Publishing LLC, New York, New York, at 1-877-980-4450.

Printed in the United States of America

Find us on

CONTENTS

Horse Families

A young horse is called a foal for the first year of its life. From the time foals are born, they need a lot of care to make sure they're healthy.

A foal starts walking less than an hour after it's born. At first, foals are very **clumsy**. This is because their legs are almost as long as they'll be when they're fully grown adult horses!

A mother horse is called
a dam. A foal stays close to its
mother for the first few weeks
of its life. Its mother keeps it
safe from other animals
and people.

A foal and its mother know each other by the sounds they make with their voices. If a foal isn't close to its mother, the mother can make a sound for the foal to find her.

The Life of a Foal

Foals have **adapted** over many years. They have large eyes that are far back on their head. Their eyes let them see danger coming from either side, not just from the front. Then, they can run away if they have to.

13

Foals drink milk for the first 10 days of their life. Then, they start eating grass and hay. They're also given special food so they'll grow up healthy. Horses have strong teeth to help them chew grass and other foods.

15

Foals use their eyes and ears to **communicate** with each other. If they see food, they can let other horses know where it is! They can point their ears and look at where the food is to show the other horses.

Foals and adult horses need
a lot of exercise. They need
to move as much as they can.
The best exercise for them
is slow and even walking.
It's good for them to
run fast sometimes too!

Horses and People

Foals live around the world. Many foals live on farms with people. There are some places you can visit to meet a foal. When you meet a foal, go toward its left and front side so it can see you.

When you meet a foal or adult horse, you need to be **gentle**. Talk softly to it so it knows you're there. Slowly reach out and let it smell your hand. If the foal touches your hand, you may pet it.

23

WORDS TO KNOW

adapted: Changed in order to live better in a certain place.

clumsy: Likely to fall or have other problems while moving.

communicate: To share ideas, thoughts, and feelings with words or by moving the body.

gentle: Soft and quiet.

INDEX

24